Nursery Rhyme
NATIVITIES

Barnabas
for
Children®

Barnabas for Children® is a registered word mark and the logo is a registered device mark of The Bible Reading Fellowship.

Text copyright © Brian Ogden 2002
Illustrations copyright © Marie Allen 2002

The author asserts the moral right
to be identified as the author of this work

Published by
The Bible Reading Fellowship
15 The Chambers, Vineyard
Abingdon, OX14 3FE
United Kingdom
Tel: + 44 (0)1865 319700
Email: enquiries@brf.org.uk
Website: www.brf.org.uk
BRF is a Registered Charity

ISBN 978 0 85746 067 7

First published 2002
This edition published 2011
Reprinted 2015
10 9 8 7 6 5 4 3 2 1

A catalogue record for this book is available from the British Library

Printed by Lightning Source

Nursery Rhyme
NATIVITIES

Three easy-to-perform plays for pre-school and early years learning

BRIAN OGDEN

This book is dedicated to the children and staff of Fakenham Infant and Nursery School in thanks for their encouragement to write the plays and the enjoyment they gave in performing them.

CONTENTS

FOREWORD

In a typically generous Brian Ogden way, the very first Nursery Rhyme Nativity came to be with Brian saying to Jane—one of our Reception teachers—'I'll write one for you!' Jane hadn't asked for this, it just came from a casual remark about what the Nursery and Reception children might perform for Christmas. So that year we premièred *Old Uncle Sam* and then, the following year, *The Christmas Three*. It was thrilling to share the fun of the children's learning of the piece and the wonderful enjoyment of the parents and families at the very special performances.

Brian has balanced the three playlets with just the right amount of religion, humour and respect. He writes with a clear understanding of good learning for children in the Foundation Stage and at Key Stage One. His able writing gives teachers the flexibility to interpret widely, something we really appreciate in Fakenham Infant and Nursery School.

This little trilogy will become a wonderful resource for teachers who want to make the Christmas performance meaningful and contemporary. The accompanying music scores and craft templates help to make the work of preparation manageable. The clever use of nursery rhyme tunes and some well-known songs give precious nursery rhymes a new lease of life. It also gives performers and audience alike an opportunity to join in easily with gusto and joy.

Brian, a special word to you—thank you, it was great to be in at the beginning.

To colleagues in Early Years settings, you have something good to look forward to. Enjoy *Uncle Sam*, *Completing the Crib* and *The Christmas Three*.

Rosine Hunt

INTRODUCTION

This book contains three separate nativity plays for use with pre-school, Reception/Foundation and Year One children. In each play the stories are told through narration and song. It is assumed that the children will mime the story alongside the narration and songs.

NARRATORS

The narration in each play is fundamental. It is essential that those chosen to narrate are very able readers with voices that are sufficiently powerful for the occasion. Working with young children, the timing of the narration is also crucial. Unless there are older children who can fulfil these requirements, it is better to use adult narrators.

THE SONGS

The songs are all written to popular tunes, mostly nursery rhymes, which will be familiar to the children. The words of the songs will need to be made available to all attending the presentation of these plays, either on a printed word sheet or on overhead projector (OHP) acetates. For ease of photocopying, a complete set of the songs may be found in Appendix One of this book. The participation of the audience is a vital aspect of the plays. It not only adds to the overall enjoyment but also encourages and supports the children.

Simple scores of the tunes used for the songs can be found in Appendix Two. Many of the songs are interchangeable between plays, so if one song appeals more than another, an exchange can be made.

In addition to the songs written for the plays, traditional Christmas carols may also be included. It may be appropriate, for example, for well-known carols to be sung to introduce and conclude a performance.

THE CHILDREN

These plays are designed to involve any number of children. If there are few children, there will be no difficulty in giving acting parts to all the children. If numbers are higher, there are many characters for whom there are no set limits—for example, shepherds, angels, innkeepers, Roman soldiers, crowds, sheep and so on. If numbers are too large to involve all the children, then a choir can make a very valuable addition. It may be that the older children in the school can fulfil this role.

STAGING

Circumstances vary enormously but provision should be made for movement on and off the acting area, together with a passageway through the audience to indicate longer distances travelled —for example, Mary and Joseph travelling from Nazareth to Bethlehem, the wise men coming from the east, and so on. Any movement by characters in the plays is indicated by the use of italics in the stage directions. There should not be any problem in staging these plays in school halls, churches or any large room.

STARTING OFF

Although some licence has obviously been taken in writing these plays, they are intended to introduce children and adults to, or remind them of, the Christmas story. There is a great opportunity, when introducing the parts of the play to the children, to show them the origin of the story by reading a section of it from the Bible. This need be no more than a few verses. Both the Good News Bible and the Contemporary English Version are suitable translations for use with children. The passages that cover the stories in the plays are Luke 1:26–38, Luke 2:1–20 and Matthew 2:1–2, 9–12.

FINAL COMMENT

These plays are designed to be fun to perform, and this should be achieved without a huge amount of preparation. Strong adult participation in the singing will enable the children to concentrate on the acting and create a sense of involvement. Any nativity play is, in itself, an act of worship and you may wish to end the presentation with a prayer. The following may be used at the end of any of these three plays.

Heavenly Father, thank you for sending Jesus into the world. Help us, this and every Christmas, to remember that it is the birth of your Son that brings true happiness. As we have recalled the events of his birth, so may we worship him throughout our lives. Amen.

COSTUME AND PROPS

Decisions over costumes and props must be left to individual users. The most important aspect must always be the safety of the children, especially regarding the length of any garments worn. Much can be done with the use of simple masks, and suggestions for these are given in the individual plays. Props are also suggested in the plays.

CHILDREN'S WORK

The introduction to the second play, 'Completing the crib', suggests ways in which the children's craft work can be incorporated within the drama, for example, making simple puppets, or a frieze. This provides an opportunity for others to see and endorse what the children have contributed themselves to the Christmas story.

OLD UNCLE
SAM

CAST AND PROPS

in order of appearance

Narrator 1
Narrator 2
Uncle Sam, dressed as a shepherd with a crook
Bag to be packed by Uncle Sam
Ten lambs (masks and tails will be sufficient)*
Rock for lamb to hide behind (a large painted
   cardboard box)
Star (child carrying a star on a stick)*
Other shepherds, with crooks
Angels, dressed in white
Mary and Joseph
Manger and baby doll
At least three wise men
Three gifts in brightly coloured boxes
Pages, who will carry gifts for wise men
Other stars (as above, but children with stars
   can lead each wise man)
* See Appendix Three for mask and star templates

Open the play with a traditional carol and welcome.

Narrator 1 Once upon a Christmas time, many years ago, there was an old shepherd called Samuel. Samuel and his friends looked after all the sheep on the hills above the town of Bethlehem.

Enter Uncle Sam with a shepherd's crook.

Narrator 2 The other shepherds called the old shepherd Uncle Sam. Uncle Sam had ten lambs that he loved dearly. Uncle Sam liked to count his lambs to make sure they were all there.

Ten lambs walk in front of Uncle Sam as he counts them. The lambs sing 'Baa, baa, black sheep' and make counting difficult.

Narrator 1 He counted them in the afternoon…

Ten lambs come back again as he counts them.

Narrator 2 …and he counted them before he went to sleep.

Ten lambs walk in front of Uncle Sam as he counts them.

Narrator 1 He counted them in the morning…

The tenth lamb goes off to hide behind a rock, some distance from the acting area.

Uncle Sam (*counts*) One, two, three, four, five, six, seven, eight, nine… er, nine. Oh no! One is missing!

After a pause he counts them again.

Uncle Sam One, two, three, four, five, six, seven, eight, nine… er, nine. Oh no! One really is missing. I must find it.

★ SONG ONE ★

Sam's song

(*Tune: Little Bo Peep*)

Old Uncle Sam has lost a lamb,
And no one knows where to find it.
Early today,
It went astray,
Wagging its tail behind it.

Uncle Sam gets his crook and packs a bag. As the next verse starts, he sets off to look for the lamb.

Old Uncle Sam has lost a lamb,
And off he goes to find it,
It fell off a rock,
And had a bad shock,
And hurt its poor tail behind it.

The lost lamb is seen behind a rock.

Old Uncle Sam has lost a lamb,
And still he's trying to find it,
He's travelled so far,
When he hears a 'baa'
From a rock—the lamb is behind it.

Uncle Sam finds the lamb and puts his arm round it.

Old Uncle Sam has found his lamb,
But lost his way on the hill tops,
Uncle Sam doesn't know
Which way to go,
But high in the sky a star stops.

Child with star leads Sam and the lamb back to the flock.

Old Uncle Sam has found his lamb,
He carries it home delighted,
There'll be party fun,
When all's said and done,
And everyone is invited.

Uncle Sam and lamb wave to other shepherds as they enter. Other shepherds wave back and then see angels coming. They stop waving and look rather frightened.

Old Uncle Sam, carrying his lamb,
Follows the star very slowly.
It leads to the flock,
Uncle Sam has a shock,
For there are some angels holy.

Star stops by shepherds. Angels come on.

The song of the sheep

(Tune: Twinkle, twinkle, little star)

To be sung twice. Sheep say loudly, 'baa, baa, baa!'

Twinkle, twinkle, little star,
Frightened sheep go 'baa, baa, baa',
Up above the sky so bright,
Letting in God's heavenly light.
Twinkle, twinkle, little star,
Now we know just what you are.

Narrator 2 Angels are messengers. They have come with a wonderful message for the shepherds. A very special baby has been born in Bethlehem. He is Jesus—the son of God.

★ SONG THREE ★

The song of the angels

(Tune: Bunessan—'Morning has broken')

Angels are singing,
God's message bringing,
Down to the shepherds,
Terrified men!
Don't be afraid now,
Don't even ask how,
Jesus is coming,
To Bethlehem.

There in a stable,
If you are able,
You'll find the baby
Warm in the straw.
Lies in a manger,
No more a stranger,
God's Son lies sleeping.
Kneel and adore.

Angels are leaving,
Shepherds, believing
All that they told them,
Go to the town.
Through all the dark streets,
Far from the flock's bleats,
There to the stable
Shepherds rush down.

Angels and star leave. Shepherds discuss who should stay behind to look after the sheep. If there are insufficient shepherds, each may speak twice.

Shepherd 1 I want to go…
Shepherd 2 So do I…
Shepherd 3 And me too…
Shepherd 4 I'm not staying here…
Shepherd 5 I'm coming with you…
Shepherd 6 So am I…
Shepherd 7 I'm going to Bethlehem…
Shepherd 8 I wouldn't miss it…
Shepherd 9 Let's go, then!
Uncle Sam But what about the sheep? Who's going to look after the sheep?

All shepherds point at Uncle Sam.

All shepherds You are!

Shepherds leave, with Uncle Sam looking fed up, sighing with his hands on his hips.

The song of the shepherds

(Tune: Here we go round the mulberry bush)

Shepherds go down to Bethlehem,
Bethlehem, Bethlehem,
Shepherds go down to Bethlehem,
On Christmas Day in the morning.

Mary, Joseph and baby come on stage and create nativity scene with the manger.

Jesus was born in Bethlehem,
Bethlehem, Bethlehem,
Jesus was born in Bethlehem,
On Christmas Day in the morning.

Shepherds reach Mary and Joseph and the baby.

Shepherds find Jesus in Bethlehem,
Bethlehem, Bethlehem,
Shepherds find Jesus in Bethlehem,
On Christmas Day in the morning.

Shepherds kneel in front of Mary, Joseph and baby.

Worship the baby in Bethlehem,
Bethlehem, Bethlehem,
Worship the baby in Bethlehem
On Christmas Day in the morning.

The song 'Away in a manger' may be sung at this point as an act of worship, or silence may be kept. Then sing last verse of the song of the shepherds.

Back to the hills by Bethlehem,
Bethlehem, Bethlehem,
Back to the hills by Bethlehem,
Go the shepherds on Christmas morning.

Shepherds leave.

Narrator 1 But the shepherds weren't the only people who were looking for Jesus at Christmas. Some wise men had come on a long journey from a faraway country. They had been following the same star for months. They brought gifts for Jesus.

Wise men, each with one or more pages carrying the gifts, walk to the acting area as the following song is sung. Each member of the wise men's party can be led by a child as a star to give extra parts if required.

The song of the wise men

(Tune: Twinkle, twinkle, little star)

Twinkle, twinkle, little star,
Leading wise men from afar,
Up above the sky so bright,
Letting in the heavenly light.
Twinkle, twinkle, little star,
Now we know just what you are.

The wise men and pages stop and look at Mary, Joseph and the baby.

13

Twinkle, twinkle, little star,
Stable door is now ajar,
Up above the sky so bright,
Letting in the heavenly light.
Twinkle, twinkle, little star,
Now we know just what you are.

Joseph accepts the gifts one by one from the wise men as the next verse is sung.

Twinkle, twinkle, little star,
Wise men offer gifts from far,
Up above the sky so bright,
Letting in the heavenly light.
Twinkle, twinkle, little star,
Now we know just what you are.

Wise men stand one side of Mary, Joseph and the baby, and the shepherds return to stand on the other side. Uncle Sam comes on with the ten lambs and stands at the back. He has his arm round one of the lambs.

★ SONG SIX ★
....

The song of the nativity

(Tune: Three blind mice)

Three wise men, three wise men,
See how they ride, see how they ride,
They bring their gifts for Jesus the king,

The shepherds heard the angels sing,
All went to the stable to see the king.
Uncle Sam, don't hide!

Shepherds push Uncle Sam to the front with one of the lambs.

Three kind gifts, three kind gifts,
That's what they bring, that's what they bring.
More gold than any of us could buy,
Frankincense for the king on high,
And myrrh for one that is to die,
That's what they bring.

Three more gifts, three more gifts,
What shall we bring? What shall we bring?
A lamb is what Uncle Sam will bring,
Our love we give to this baby king,
We bring our lives and our faith in him,
That's what we bring.

Narrator 2   The wise men started on their long journey home. Mary and Joseph were warned that Herod the king wanted to take baby Jesus away from them. They went on a secret journey to Egypt so that they could keep Jesus safe. The shepherds went back to the hills overlooking the town of Bethlehem.

All leave. Uncle Sam comes on with nine lambs. The shepherds creep on behind him and stand around Uncle Sam. He is counting his lambs.

Uncle Sam   (*counts*) One, two, three, four, five, six, seven, eight, nine… er, nine.

All shepherds And this time he knows where the missing one is!

End the play with a carol or song, and prayer.

COMPLETING THE CRIB

INTRODUCTION

This play can be treated in two ways. It can be used as it stands, as with the other two Nursery Rhyme Nativity plays, or it can be used to include craft work that the children have produced. To use it straight, ignore the instructions for the inclusion of craft work and follow the script as given.

INCLUDING CHILDREN'S CRAFT WORK

Puppet figures

Using the templates in Appendix Three on page 59, make puppet figures to be placed in a large sand tray as the play evolves. The figures will correspond to the characters in the play, and will be moved in and out by the narrators.

Overhead projector acetates

Using the outlines in this book, the children draw or colour the figures in the play. The figures can be projected as the play evolves.

Continuous frieze

As a way of introducing the Christmas story to the children, let them draw or colour and cut out the characters in the story. The characters can be mounted, together with some basic scenery, on a continuous frieze, and the frieze unwound to show the appropriate part of the story as the play develops. If the acting area is wide enough, the whole length can be displayed.

If the frieze is too long, or management of it is too complicated, show only the part that corresponds to the part of the play currently being acted. To do this, mount the beginning and end of the frieze on lengths of dowel (or broom handles). Slot one end of each dowel into holes drilled in a heavy piece of wood that lies on the floor. As the top of the dowel is turned, so the frieze progresses.

In the script below, the boxes show when to move the puppets in and out of the sand tray. The same timings apply to showing figures on the OHP or displaying the relevant section of a frieze.

> *Place the figures of Mary and then the angel in the sand tray.*

Mary enters, followed by the angel.

Narrator 1 Our story begins in the village of Nazareth two thousand years ago. Mary was at home sweeping the floor. Suddenly, through the dust she saw someone standing there. At first she thought it must be Joseph, her husband-to-be. As she looked closer, she knew it wasn't Joseph. In fact, the figure didn't look like anyone she knew.

Narrator 2 'Peace be with you, Mary. God has greatly blessed you.'

Narrator 1 Mary was very frightened. She knew this was an angel. Angels were God's messengers. Surely he hadn't got a message for her!

Narrator 2 'Don't be afraid, Mary. I've come from God to tell you that you are going to have a baby son. You will call him Jesus. He will be great and will be called the Son of God.'

Narrator 1 Mary could hardly believe what the angel told her. She had been chosen by God to be the mother of his Son. But there were to be hard times, as well as good times, ahead for Mary.

The angel, and then Mary, slowly leave the acting area as the following song is sung.

> *Remove the figures from the tray as the song is sung.*

★ SONG ONE ★

Mary's song

(Tune: London Bridge is falling down)

The angel came to Mary's home,
Mary's home, Mary's home.
The angel came to Mary's home,
In the morning.

Mary wondered why he came,
Why he came, why he came.
Mary wondered why he came,
In the morning.

'The Lord God has chosen you,
Chosen you, chosen you,
The Lord God has chosen you,
This fine morning.'

'You'll be mother to his son,
To his son, to his son.
You'll be mother to his son,
Precious baby.'

'He will lead us back to God,
Back to God, back to God,
He will lead us back to God,
Precious baby.'

'Let it happen as you will,
As you will, as you will.
Let it happen as you will.'
So said Mary.

> *Add figures showing a crowd of people,*
> *including Mary and Joseph, to the tray as*
> *the song ends.*

Villagers, Mary, Joseph and a Roman soldier enter.

Narrator 1 Only a few months after the angel
had visited Mary, the people of
Nazareth had a surprise. A Roman
soldier marched into the village.
The villagers came to hear what
he said.

Narrator 2 'Augustus, your noble Emperor, has
ordered everyone to go to their
family towns to be counted. You
must start out tomorrow.'

Narrator 1 Mary and Joseph knew that they
would have to travel from Nazareth
to Bethlehem. Bethlehem was
David's town and they belonged to
David's family. It was a journey of
many miles and Mary was going to
have her baby. They wouldn't be able
to travel quickly. Mary packed her
things and Joseph fed the donkey.

> *During the singing of this song, place Mary,*
> *Joseph and the donkey in the sand tray.*

Mary and Joseph start their journey.

★ SONG TWO ★

The song of the donkey

(Tune: Baa, baa, black sheep)

Donkey, donkey,
With your precious load,
Trotting slowly
Up the road.
Many miles to travel
To David's town,
Now you're trotting up the hill,
Soon be trotting down.

Donkey, donkey,
With your precious load,
Trotting slowly
Up the road.
Not far to go now,
The town's in sight,
You can take it easier
Later tonight.

Donkey, donkey,
With your precious load,
Trotting slowly
Up the road.
The town is very crowded,
Lots of people there,
Mary and Joseph are
Starting to despair.

Donkey, donkey,
With your precious load,
Trotting slowly
Up the road.
All the inns are full,
No rooms are free,
Jesus has a stable for
His nursery.

> *At the end of the song, place the innkeepers in the sand tray along with Mary and Joseph.*

Mary and Joseph watch as the innkeepers enter, singing and dancing.

★ SONG THREE ★

The song of the innkeepers

(Sung twice to the tune of Hokey Cokey)

We've put the full signs out,
The vacant signs in,
In, out, in, out,
Full without a doubt.
We're making loads of money,
It's enough to make us shout,
And that's what it's all about!
All our inns are full now,
All our inns are full now,
All our inns are full now,
That's why we sing and shout!

Narrator 1 So Mary and Joseph reach Bethlehem only to find that everyone has got there before them. All the inns are full. There doesn't seem to be anywhere for them to go. And then a kind innkeeper tells them that they can use his stable.

Narrator 2 It's there that Mary gives birth to Jesus, the Son of God. Not a royal palace for the son of the King of kings—just a humble stable. But there's love in that stable—the love of God who sent his Son, and the love of Mary who cared for him.

The innkeepers leave. Mary and Joseph walk off and return at once with Mary carrying the baby, which she places in some straw.

> *Remove the innkeepers and, as the next song is sung, place the figure of the baby in the sand tray with Mary and Joseph.*

★ SONG FOUR ★

Lullaby

(Sung softly to the tune of Frère Jacques)

Baby's sleeping, baby's sleeping,
In the straw, in the straw,
Angel's promise keeping,
Angel's promise keeping,
Son of God, Son of God.

Baby's sleeping, baby's sleeping,
In the straw, in the straw,
Joseph now is peeping,
Joseph now is peeping,
Full of joy, full of joy.

Baby's sleeping, baby's sleeping,
In the straw, in the straw,
Mary now is weeping,
Mary now is weeping,
Tears of joy, tears of joy.

> ***Remove the figures of Mary, Joseph and the baby from the sand tray.***

Mary, Joseph and the baby leave as the narrator introduces the shepherds.

Narrator 1 As baby Jesus sleeps soundly in the stable, some shepherds on the hills above Bethlehem have a surprise.

> ***Place shepherds and sheep in the sand tray.***

Shepherds enter.

(During the singing of Song Five, the angels will appear to the shepherds.)

The song of the shepherds and angels

(Tune: There's a hole in my bucket)

If there is a choir, they should sing alternate verses. The audience may also do the same. The shepherds should be in two groups to alternate the verses.

There's a sheep gone a-missing,
A-missing, a-missing,
There's a sheep gone a-missing,
Dear Aaron, a sheep.

Then find it, dear Reuben,
Dear Reuben, dear Reuben,
Then find it, dear Reuben,
Dear Reuben, find it.

But it's night-time, dear Aaron,
Dear Aaron, dear Aaron,
It's night-time, dear Aaron,
I'm afraid of the dark.

There's a light shining brightly,
Dear Reuben, dear Reuben,
There's a light shining brightly,
It's dazzling us all.

> ***Add angels to the sand tray.***

Angels enter.

It's an angel, dear Aaron,
Dear Aaron, dear Aaron,
It's an angel, dear Aaron,
With a message from God.

The next two verses should be sung by the angels.

Now listen, dear shepherds,
Dear shepherds, dear shepherds,
Now listen, dear shepherds,
To our message from God.

There's a baby, dear shepherds,
Dear shepherds, dear shepherds,
There's a baby, dear shepherds,
The true Son of God.

The next verse should be sung by the shepherds.

And where shall we find him,
Dear angels, dear angels,
And where shall we find him,
The true Son of God?

The next verse should be sung by the angels.

He lies in a stable,
Dear shepherds, dear shepherds,
He lies in a stable.
Go worship him there.

The next three verses should be sung by everyone.

There's some shepherds gone a-missing,
A-missing, a-missing,
There's some shepherds gone a-missing,
They've run to the town.

In the stable is Jesus,
Is Jesus, is Jesus,
In the stable is Jesus,
The dear Son of God.

The shepherds now worship,
Now worship, now worship,
The shepherds now worship
The dear Son of God.

Remove shepherds from sand tray.

Shepherds leave.

Narrator 1 The shepherds returned to the hills and to their sheep. They were the first people to see Jesus.

Narrator 2 But Jesus had some more special visitors. These were men who had travelled from the East. They were astrologers who studied the stars.

Narrator 1 A star had led them from their own country to Bethlehem. They were looking for a child who they believed would become a great leader.

Place wise men and servants in sand tray.

Wise men process together with servants carrying gifts.

★ SONG SIX ★

The song of the wise men

(Tune: Three blind mice)

Three wise men, three wise men,
See how they ride, see how they ride.
They all ride after the star so bright,
That leads them westwards every night,
They've never seen such a brilliant light—
Those three wise men.

Three wise men, three wise men,
See how they ride, see how they ride.
They find the stable and infant king,
And kneel before him, worshipping,
And to him three precious gifts they bring,
Those three wise men.

Three wise men, three wise men,
See how they ride, see how they ride.
The first presents his gift of gold,
To the king of whom it was foretold
He would give his life for young and old—
The Son of God.

Three wise men, three wise men,
See how they ride, see how they ride.
The second offers incense rare,
A symbol of a priestly prayer,
To one who all our wrong will share—
The Son of God.

Three wise men, three wise men,
See how they ride, see how they ride.
Myrrh is the gift from wise man three,
A sweet perfume from an Arabian tree,
For Jesus at his nativity—
The Son of God.

Remove all the figures from the sand tray.

The wise men go off in one direction and Mary, Joseph and the baby in another.

Narrator 1 The wise men rode back home— wiser because they both looked for and found Jesus.

Narrator 2 Just as our story started in Nazareth, so it ends there too. Mary, Joseph and Jesus went for a time to live in Egypt. Later they returned to Nazareth where Jesus grew up. He worked in the carpenter's shop with Joseph until the time came when he left home to begin the work that God, his Father, had sent him to do.

End the play with a carol or song, and prayer.

THE

CHRISTMAS

THREE

INTRODUCTION

This play uses three main speaking parts, Dorcas the donkey, Woolly the sheep and Kasbah the camel. If the children playing the parts of these three characters are too young, the speeches can be read by adult narrators in their place.

CAST AND PROPS

in order of appearance

Narrator 1 for introduction
Narrator 2 (to read Dorcas' part if child is too young to do so)
Narrator 3 (to read Woolly's part if child is too young to do so)
Narrator 4 (to read Kasbah's part if child is too young to do so)
Dorcas the donkey, wearing donkey mask*
Woolly the sheep, wearing sheep mask*
Kasbah the camel, wearing camel mask*
Mary
The angel
Roman soldiers, one with proclamation parchment

Citizens of Nazareth, with tools of trade—brushes and so on
Joseph
Innkeepers, wearing aprons
Doll and manger
Shepherds with crooks
Sheep
Choir of angels
Star hung high above acting area
Wise men (minimum of three, maybe more)
Gifts for the wise men
Pages for wise men, if required

* See Appendix Three for mask templates

Narrator 1 Many years ago, at what we now call Christmas time, three animals met in a field just outside the town of Bethlehem. First there was Dorcas the donkey.

Animals enter as each is introduced.

Dorcas/ Narrator 2
I'm just a grey donkey,
With one ear that's wonky,
My home is in old Nazareth.
I carried young Mary
On a journey quite hairy,
To where Jesus drew his first breath.

Narrator 1 Then there was Woolly the sheep.

Woolly/ Narrator 3
I'm Woolly, not Wolly,
Nor Molly or Polly,
I live on the hills very high.
One night when asleep,
Something frightened us sheep,
As a large choir of angels flew by.

Narrator 1 And last, but not least, there was Kasbah the camel.

Kasbah/ Narrator 4
I'm a camel called Kasbah,
Who followed a bright star,
Not turning from hardship and danger.
My master's one of the wise men,
But imagine my surprise when
He gave gifts to a child in a manger.

Dorcas/ Narrator 2 It's quite amazing, but I think that we three are all part of the same wonderful story—the story of the first Christmas ever. I was the donkey that took Mary to Bethlehem, where she had her baby.

Woolly/ Narrator 3 I was one of the sheep that saw the angels who told the shepherds about the baby in Bethlehem.

Kasbah/ Narrator 4 And I was the camel who brought one of the wise men to worship the baby in Bethlehem. Perhaps, Dorcas, you should tell us how your part of the story started.

Dorcas/ Narrator 2 It all began far away in the village of Nazareth. Nazareth is my home, and Joseph, the village carpenter, is my master. Joseph was going to be

married to Mary. One day Mary had a very unexpected visitor.

During the song, Mary and the angel enter. Mary kneels as she sees the angel.

★ SONG ONE ★

The song of Mary and the angel

(Tune: Ring-a-ring o' roses)

Sing a song of Mary,
Had a visit scary.
An angel! An angel!
Mary knelt down.

God has sent his angel
To visit Mary humble.
An angel! An angel!
Mary knelt down.

'Mary, do not fear me,
You will have a baby.'
An angel! An angel!
Mary knelt down.

'He'll be born at Christmas,
You will name him Jesus.'
An angel! An angel!
Mary knelt down.

Mary did agree then,
She said, 'Let it be, then.'
An angel! An angel!
Mary knelt down.

Angel went away then,
Mary went to pray then.
An angel! An angel!
Mary knelt down.

The angel leaves, followed a few moments later by Mary.

Dorcas/ Narrator 2 Mary had been chosen by God to be the mother of Jesus. But this didn't

mean that everything was going to easy—far from it. Not long before the baby was due to be born, someone else arrived in Nazareth. It was a Roman soldier with some bad news for Mary and Joseph. They were going to have to make a long journey—all the way from Nazareth to Bethlehem.

During the song, Roman soldiers enter and enact the proclamation to the citizens of Nazareth, including Mary and Joseph. By the end, Mary and Joseph are seen on their journey.

★ SONG TWO ★

The song of the Roman soldiers

(Tune: The grand old Duke of York)

O the Emperor of Rome,
He had so many men,
He sent them up to the top of the hills,
And he sent them down again.
And when they were up,
they were up;
And when they were down,
they were down;
And even if they were halfway up,
They visited every town.

O the Emperor of Rome,
He ordered everyone
To leave their homes and go at once,
To be counted one by one.
And when they were up,
they were up,
And when they were down,
they were down,
And even if they were halfway up,
They went to their family town.

So then Joseph came to me,
Said, 'It's time to pack.'
He walked us up to the top of the hills,
With Mary on my back.

And when we were up,
we were up,
And when we were down,
we were down,
And after many a dusty mile,
We came to Bethlehem town.

Woolly/ Narrator 3 That sounds like quite a journey you made, Dorcas.

Dorcas/ Narrator 2 It certainly was—up and down the hills and along the dusty roads. I was trying to keep Mary as comfortable as possible. I wanted her to have her baby in Bethlehem and not on the way.

Kasbah/ Narrator 4 So did you get to Bethlehem in time for the baby to be born there?

Dorcas/ Narrator 2 Yes, we did, but because we had to travel slowly everyone else got there before us. The town, as you know, was full of people coming to be counted. There was nowhere left for us to stay. Poor Joseph was so worried.

Innkeepers enter from one side and Mary and Joseph from the other.

The song of the innkeepers

(Tune: Sing a song of sixpence)

Sing a song of travellers,
There are no empty beds,
Mary and Joseph have nowhere
To lay their weary heads.
When the beds are taken
We all start to sing,
Think of all the lovely cash
That all these travellers bring.

Sing a song of inns full,
Guests are everywhere.
You've arrived too late, mate,
We're full right up to here!
All the space is taken,
The outlook is quite black.
The only place that's empty is—
A stable round the back.

During the following narration, the innkeeper shows Mary and Joseph into the stable area. Mary lifts a doll from some straw and Mary and Joseph stand looking at the baby.

Dorcas/ Narrator 2 So Joseph and Mary followed the innkeeper into the stable. It was like a cave cut into the hillside at the back of the inn. Soon after that, Mary gave birth to Jesus. I was there; I heard the first cries that Jesus made. I saw the look on Mary and Joseph's faces—they were so happy.

Kasbah/ Narrator 4 It must have been a truly wonderful moment—the birth of that very special baby.

Silence is kept for a moment. If space makes it necessary, Mary and Joseph leave—otherwise Mary and Joseph remain to one side as the attention turns to the shepherds.

During the following narration, shepherds, sheep and one angel enter. There's a fuss as the sheep are rounded up.

Woolly/ Narrator 3 I'm sure it was at the same time that our shepherds and we sheep saw our angel. At first there was one angel. He told us that a special baby had been born today in Bethlehem. Then the whole sky seemed full of angels, all singing a wonderful song.

The choir of angels enter, singing the song.

The song of the angels

(Tune: Michael row the boat ashore)

Chorus:
Come and praise the Lord in heaven,
Hallelujah,
Come and praise the Lord in heaven,
Hallelujah.

Peace on earth to everyone, Hallelujah,
Brilliant news of God's own Son, Hallelujah.

Chorus

In a stable in the town, Hallelujah,
God Almighty has come down, Hallelujah.

Chorus

Lying on a bed of straw, Hallelujah,
Jesus, Saviour evermore, Hallelujah.

Chorus

All the angels joined in praise, Hallelujah,
The first of all our Christmas Days, Hallelujah.

Chorus

Shepherds left their frightened sheep, Hallelujah.
Ran fast down the hillside steep, Hallelujah.

Chorus

Found the baby promised there, Hallelujah.
Safe in Mary's tender care, Hallelujah.

Chorus

Worshipped Jesus, God's own Son, Hallelujah.
Went back telling everyone, Hallelujah.

Chorus

Dorcas/ Narrator 2 Seeing all those angels must have been very frightening.

During the following narration, the shepherds leave the sheep and run off, reappearing in the stable scene. The angels also leave.

Woolly/ Narrator 3 Yes, it was. All us sheep went quite baa-my! I think the shepherds were just as scared as we were. They left one shepherd to look after us and the others ran down to the town. I heard them telling him about it later.

Dorcas/ Narrator 2 I remember when they arrived. They were all out of breath. They burst into the stable and then went very quiet. They saw the baby Jesus and knelt down around the manger.

★ SONG FIVE ★

The song of the shepherds

(Tune: Kum ba yah)

The song is sung by all as an act of worship.
He is Christ the Lord, worship him,
He is Christ the Lord, worship him,
He is Christ the Lord, worship him,
Come now and worship him.

He's the Son of God, worship him,
He's the Son of God, worship him,
He's the Son of God, worship him,
Come now and worship him.

He's our Saviour now, worship him,
He's our Saviour now, worship him,
He's our Saviour now, worship him,
Come now and worship him.

The shepherds stand at the end of the song and pretend to speak to Mary and Joseph.

Dorcas/ Narrator 2 One of the shepherds told Mary and Joseph what the angel had said about the baby. They looked very surprised. You could see it made Mary think.

During the following narration, the shepherds run back to their sheep.

Woolly/ Narrator 3 Seeing Jesus made the shepherds think, as well. We could hear them as they came back up the hill. They talked about it for days. But what about you, Kasbah? You've been standing there patiently listening to us. Tell us what happened to you.

During the following narration, Kasbah's master enters, obviously looking heavenwards. If possible, a star should be hung appropriately.

Kasbah/ Narrator 4 My story starts with a star. My master is an astrologer, a man who studies the stars. One night he saw a new star. My master believed that this star meant that someone very special would be born. He and some friends made up their minds to follow the star and find the special person.

During the singing of this song, Kasbah and friends set out on their journey.

★ SONG SIX ★

The song of the star

(Tune: This old man)

Superstar, led us west,
To the town that God has blessed.
With the bright star guiding all the way—
To Jesus born on Christmas Day.

Superstar, leading on,
Never mind the burning sun.
With the bright star guiding all the way—
To Jesus born on Christmas Day.

Superstar, in the sky,
Cross the desert very dry.
With the bright star guiding all the way—
To Jesus born on Christmas Day.

Superstar stopped at last,
Above the baby long forecast.
The bright star led us all the way—
To Jesus born on Christmas Day.

Years have passed, but it's true,
Stars still shine for me and you.
It doesn't matter who you are,
Jesus can be your Superstar.

Kasbah/ Narrator 4 My master and his friends followed the star from our home in the east. We had many adventures on the way. We crossed high mountains and dry deserts. After many days the star stopped over Bethlehem. It was here that my master found the special person for whom he was searching.

Woolly/ Narrator 3 And the special person was the baby that the shepherds found.

Dorcas/ Narrator 2 The baby whose mother I had carried here.

Kasbah/ Narrator 4 Yes, we all came here because of Jesus, the baby of Bethlehem. My master and his friends brought presents for Jesus.

During the singing of this song, the wise men, plus pages if required, process round until they kneel before Mary, Joseph and the baby. There they offer their gifts.

The song of the wise men

(Tune: Kum bah yah)

Wise men worshipped him, Christ the Lord,
Wise men worshipped him, Christ the Lord,
Wise men worshipped him, Christ the Lord,
Come now and worship him.

Gave their gifts to him, Christ the Lord,
Gave their gifts to him, Christ the Lord,
Gave their gifts to him, Christ the Lord,
Come now and worship him.

At the end of the song, Joseph runs over to Dorcas and pretends to speak to her.

Dorcas/ Narrator 2 It seems I have to go. An angel has warned Joseph that King Herod's soldiers are searching for Jesus. We have to leave Bethlehem and go as quickly as possible to Egypt.

Kasbah/ Narrator 4 I must leave as well. My master and his friends are heading back east. It will be good to get home again.
I'm a camel called Kasbah,
Who followed the bright star
That led to the babe in the manger.
We went home again,
Over mountain and plain.
Thank God, for he kept us from danger.

Woolly/ Narrator 3 I must get back to the hills again with the rest of the flock. The shepherds will be wondering where I am.
I'm Woolly, not Wolly,
Nor Molly or Polly,
And I live on the hills very high.
My story ends,
Back with my friends;
With no angel choir in the sky.

Dorcas/ Narrator 2 Perhaps one day we will all discover what happens to the special baby that brought us all together.
I'm just a grey donkey,
With one ear that's wonky,
My home is in old Nazareth.
We went to the Nile,
And stayed there awhile,
Until we heard of Herod's death.

Narrator 1 The Christmas three never met again. Kasbah and the wise men returned to their homes in the east. Woolly went back to the shepherds on the hillside over Bethlehem, and Dorcas carried Mary and Jesus, along with Joseph, to safety in Egypt. And the special baby grew up to become the most famous person who had ever lived—Jesus Christ, the Son of God.

End the play with a carol or song, and prayer.

APPENDIX ONE

COMPLETE SET OF THE SONGS

OLD UNCLE SAM

★1 Sam's song

(Tune: Little Bo Peep)

Old Uncle Sam has lost a lamb,
And no one knows where to find it.
Early today,
It went astray,
Wagging its tail behind it.

Old Uncle Sam has lost a lamb
And off he goes to find it,
It fell off a rock,
And had a bad shock,
And hurt its poor tail behind it.

Old Uncle Sam has lost a lamb,
And still he's trying to find it,
He's travelled so far,
When he hears a 'baa'
From a rock—the lamb is behind it.

Old Uncle Sam has found his lamb,
But lost his way on the hill tops,
Uncle Sam doesn't know
Which way to go,
But high in the sky a star stops.

Old Uncle Sam has found his lamb,
He carries it home delighted,
There'll be party fun,
When all's said and done,
And everyone is invited.

Old Uncle Sam, carrying his lamb,
Follows the star very slowly.
It leads to the flock,
Uncle Sam has a shock,
For there are some angels holy.

⭐2 The song of the sheep

(Tune: Twinkle, twinkle, little star)

Twinkle, twinkle, little star,
Frightened sheep go 'baa, baa, baa'.
Up above the sky so bright,
Letting in God's heavenly light.
Twinkle, twinkle, little star,
Now we know just what you are.

⭐3 The song of the angels

(Tune: Bunessan—'Morning has broken')

Angels are singing,
God's message bringing,
Down to the shepherds,
Terrified men!
Don't be afraid now,
Don't even ask how,
Jesus is coming,
To Bethlehem.

Angels are leaving,
Shepherds believing
All that they told them
Go to the town.
Through all the dark streets,
Far from the flock's bleats,
There to the stable
Shepherds rush down.

There in a stable,
If you are able,
You'll find the baby
Warm in the straw.
Lies in a manger,
No more a stranger,
God's Son lies sleeping.
Kneel and adore.

4

The song of the shepherds

(Tune: Here we go round the mulberry bush)

Shepherds go down to Bethlehem,
Bethlehem, Bethlehem,
Shepherds go down to Bethlehem,
On Christmas Day in the morning.

Jesus was born in Bethlehem,
Bethlehem, Bethlehem,
Jesus was born in Bethlehem,
On Christmas Day in the morning.

Shepherds find Jesus in Bethlehem,
Bethlehem, Bethlehem,
Shepherds find Jesus in Bethlehem,
On Christmas Day in the morning.

Worship the baby in Bethlehem,
Bethlehem, Bethlehem,
Worship the baby in Bethlehem,
On Christmas Day in the morning.

Back to the hills by Bethlehem,
Bethlehem, Bethlehem,
Back to the hills by Bethlehem
Go the shepherds on Christmas morning.

★5 The song of the wise men

(Tune: Twinkle, twinkle, little star)

Twinkle, twinkle, little star,
Leading wise men from afar,
Up above the sky so bright,
Letting in the heavenly light.
Twinkle, twinkle, little star,
Now we know just what you are.

Twinkle, twinkle, little star,
Stable door is now ajar,
Up above the sky so bright,
Letting in the heavenly light.
Twinkle, twinkle, little star,
Now we know just what you are.

Twinkle, twinkle, little star,
Wise men offer gifts from far,
Up above the sky so bright,
Letting in the heavenly light.
Twinkle, twinkle, little star,
Now we know just what you are.

⭐ 6

The song of the nativity

(Tune: Three blind mice)

Three wise men, three wise men,
See how they ride, see how they ride.
They bring their gifts for Jesus the king,
The shepherds heard the angels sing,
All went to the stable to see the king.
Uncle Sam, don't hide!

Three kind gifts, three kind gifts,
That's what they bring, that's what they bring.
More gold than any of us could buy,
Frankincense for the king on high,
And myrrh for one that is to die,
That's what they bring.

Three more gifts, three more gifts,
What shall we bring? What shall we bring?
A lamb is what Uncle Sam will bring,
Our love we give to this baby king,
We bring our lives and our faith in him,
That's what we bring.

COMPLETING THE CRIB

★ 1
Mary's song

(Tune: London Bridge is falling down)

The angel came to Mary's home,
Mary's home, Mary's home.
The angel came to Mary's home,
In the morning.

Mary wondered why he came,
Why he came, why he came.
Mary wondered why he came,
In the morning.

'The Lord God has chosen you,
Chosen you, chosen you,
The Lord God has chosen you,
This fine morning.'

'You'll be mother to his son,
To his son, to his son.
You'll be mother to his son,
Precious baby.'

'He will lead us back to God,
Back to God, back to God,
He will lead us back to God,
Precious baby.'

'Let it happen as you will,
As you will, as you will.
Let it happen as you will.'
So said Mary.

★2

The song of the donkey

(Tune: Baa, baa, black sheep)

Donkey, donkey,
With your precious load,
Trotting slowly
Up the road.
Many miles to travel
To David's town,
Now you're trotting up the hill,
Soon be trotting down.

Donkey, donkey,
With your precious load,
Trotting slowly
Up the road.
Not far to go now,
The town's in sight,
You can take it easier
Later tonight.

Donkey, donkey,
With your precious load,
Trotting slowly
Up the road.
The town is very crowded,
Lots of people there,
Mary and Joseph are
Starting to despair.

Donkey, donkey,
With your precious load,
Trotting slowly
Up the road.
All the inns are full,
No rooms are free,
Jesus has a stable for
His nursery.

★3

The song of the innkeepers

(Sung twice to the tune of Hokey Cokey)

We've put the full signs out,
The vacant signs in,
In, out, in, out,
Full without a doubt.
We're making loads of money,
It's enough to make us shout,
And that's what it's all about!
All our inns are full now,
All our inns are full now,
All our inns are full now,
That's why we sing and shout!

★4

Lullaby

(Sung softly to the tune of Frère Jacques)

Baby's sleeping, baby's sleeping,
In the straw, in the straw,
Angel's promise keeping,
Angel's promise keeping,
Son of God, Son of God.

Baby's sleeping, baby's sleeping,
In the straw, in the straw,
Joseph now is peeping,
Joseph now is peeping,
Full of joy, full of joy.

Baby's sleeping, baby's sleeping,
In the straw, in the straw,
Mary now is weeping,
Mary now is weeping,
Tears of joy, tears of joy.

5

The song of the shepherds and angels

(Tune: There's a hole in my bucket)

There's a sheep gone a-missing,
A-missing, a-missing,
There's a sheep gone a-missing,
Dear Aaron, a sheep.

Then find it, dear Reuben,
Dear Reuben, dear Reuben,
Then find it, dear Reuben,
Dear Reuben, find it.

But it's night-time, dear Aaron,
Dear Aaron, dear Aaron,
It's night-time, dear Aaron,
I'm afraid of the dark.

There's a light shining brightly,
Dear Reuben, dear Reuben,
There's a light shining brightly,
It's dazzling us all.

It's an angel, dear Aaron,
Dear Aaron, dear Aaron,
It's an angel, dear Aaron,
With a message from God.

Angels:

Now listen, dear shepherds,
Dear shepherds, dear shepherds,
Now listen, dear shepherds,
To our message from God.

There's a baby, dear shepherds,
Dear shepherds, dear shepherds,
There's a baby, dear shepherds,
The true Son of God.

Shepherds:

And where shall we find him,
Dear angel, dear angel,
And where shall we find him,
The true Son of God?

Angels:

He lies in a stable,
Dear shepherds, dear shepherds,
He lies in a stable.
Go worship him there.

Everyone:

There's some shepherds gone a-missing,
A-missing, a-missing,
There's some shepherds gone a-missing,
They've run to the town.

In the stable is Jesus,
Is Jesus, is Jesus,
In the stable is Jesus,
The dear Son of God.

The shepherds now worship,
Now worship, now worship,
The shepherds now worship
The dear Son of God.

★ 6

The song of the wise men

(Tune: Three blind mice)

Three wise men, three wise men,
See how they ride, see how they ride.
They all ride after the star so bright
That leads them westwards every night,
They've never seen such a brilliant light—
Those three wise men.

Three wise men, three wise men,
See how they ride, see how they ride.
They find the stable and infant king,
And kneel before him, worshipping,
And to him three precious gifts they bring,
Those three wise men.

Three wise men, three wise men,
See how they ride, see how they ride.
The first presents his gift of gold,
To the king of whom it was foretold
He would give his life for young and old—
The Son of God.

Three wise men, three wise men,
See how they ride, see how they ride.
The second offers incense rare,
A symbol of a priestly prayer,
To one who all our wrong will share—
The Son of God.

Three wise men, three wise men,
See how they ride, see how they ride.
Myrrh is the gift from wise man three,
A sweet perfume from an Arabian tree,
For Jesus at his nativity—
The Son of God.

THE CHRISTMAS THREE

★ 1
The song of Mary and the angel

(Tune: Ring-a-ring o' roses)

Sing a song of Mary,
Had a visit scary.
An angel! An angel!
Mary knelt down.

God has sent his angel
To visit Mary humble.
An angel! An angel!
Mary knelt down.

'Mary, do not fear me,
You will have a baby.'
An angel! An angel!
Mary knelt down.

'He'll be born at Christmas,
You will name him Jesus.'
An angel! An angel!
Mary knelt down.

Mary did agree then,
She said, 'Let it be, then.'
An angel! An angel!
Mary knelt down.

Angel went away then,
Mary went to pray then.
An angel! An angel!
Mary knelt down.

⭐ 2 The song of the Roman soldiers

(Tune: The grand old Duke of York)

O the Emperor of Rome,
He had so many men,
He sent them up to the top of the hills,
And he sent them down again.
And when they were up,
they were up;
And when they were down,
they were down;
And even if they were halfway up,
They visited every town.

O the Emperor of Rome,
He ordered everyone
To leave their homes and go at once,
To be counted one by one.
And when they were up,
they were up,
And when they were down,
they were down,
And even if they were halfway up,
They went to their family town.

So then Joseph came to me,
Said, 'It's time to pack.'
He walked us up to the top of the hills,
With Mary on my back.
And when we were up,
we were up,
And when we were down,
we were down,
And after many a dusty mile,
We came to Bethlehem town.

44

The song of the innkeepers

(Tune: Sing a song of sixpence)

Sing a song of travellers,
There are no empty beds,
Mary and Joseph have nowhere
To lay their weary heads.
When the beds are taken
We all start to sing,
Think of all the lovely cash
That all these travellers bring.

Sing a song of inns full,
Guests are everywhere.
You've arrived too late, mate,
We're full right up to here!
All the space is taken,
The outlook is quite black.
The only place that's empty is—
A stable round the back.

★ 4

The song of the angels

(Tune: Michael row the boat ashore)

> **Chorus:**
> **Come and praise the Lord in heaven, Hallelujah,**
> **Come and praise the Lord in heaven, Hallelujah.**

Peace on earth to everyone,
Hallelujah,
Brilliant news of God's own Son,
Hallelujah.

Chorus

In a stable in the town,
Hallelujah,
God Almighty has come down,
Hallelujah.

Chorus

Lying on a bed of straw,
Hallelujah,
Jesus, Saviour evermore,
Hallelujah.

Chorus

All the angels joined in praise,
Hallelujah,
The first of all our Christmas
Days, Hallelujah.

Chorus

Shepherds left their frightened
sheep, Hallelujah.
Ran fast down the hillside steep,
Hallelujah.

Chorus

Found the baby promised there,
Hallelujah.
Safe in Mary's tender care,
Hallelujah.

Chorus

Worshipped Jesus, God's own Son,
Hallelujah.
Went back telling everyone,
Hallelujah.

Chorus

★5

The song of the shepherds

(Tune: Kum ba yah)

He is Christ the Lord, worship him,
He is Christ the Lord, worship him,
He is Christ the Lord, worship him,
Come now and worship him.

He's the Son of God, worship him,
He's the Son of God, worship him,
He's the Son of God, worship him,
Come now and worship him.

He's our Saviour now, worship him,
He's our Saviour now, worship him,
He's our Saviour now, worship him,
Come now and worship him.

★6★ The song of the star

(Tune: This old man)

Superstar, led us west,
To the town that God has blessed.
With the bright star guiding
   all the way—
To Jesus born on Christmas Day.

Superstar, leading on,
Never mind the burning sun.
With the bright star guiding
   all the way—
To Jesus born on Christmas Day.

Superstar, in the sky,
Cross the desert very dry.
With the bright star guiding
   all the way—
To Jesus born on Christmas Day.

Superstar stopped at last,
Above the baby long forecast.
The bright star led us all the way—
To Jesus born on Christmas Day.

Y   passed, but it's true,
Stars still shine for me and you.
It doesn't matter who you are,
Jesus can be your Superstar.

Song Five reprise: The song of the wise men

(Tune: Kum bah yah)

Wise men worshipped him, Christ the Lord,
Wise men worshipped him, Christ the Lord,
Wise men worshipped him, Christ the Lord,
Come now and worship him.

Gave their gifts to him, Christ the Lord,
Gave their gifts to him, Christ the Lord,
Gave their gifts to him, Christ the Lord,
Come now and worship him.

MUSIC SCORES FOR THE NURSERY RHYME TUNES

OLD UNCLE SAM

Song One: Sam's song

(Tune: Little Bo Peep)

Song Two: The song of the sheep

(Tune: Twinkle, twinkle, little star)

Song Three: The song of the angels

(Tune: Bunessan—'Morning has broken')

Song Four: The song of the shepherds

(Tune: Here we go round the mulberry bush)

Song Five: The song of the wise men

(Tune: Twinkle, twinkle, little star)

Song Six: The song of the nativity

(Tune: Three blind mice)

COMPLETING THE CRIB

Song One: Mary's song

(Tune: London Bridge is falling down)

Song Two: The song of the donkey

(Tune: Baa, baa, black sheep)

Song Three: The song of the innkeepers

(Sung twice to the tune of Hokey Cokey)

Song Four: Lullaby

(Sung softly to the tune of Frère Jacques)

Song Five: The song of the shepherds and angels

(Tune: There's a hole in my bucket)

Song Six: The song of the wise men

(Tune: Three blind mice)

THE CHRISTMAS THREE

Song One: The song of Mary and the angel

(Tune: Ring-a-ring o' roses)

Song Two: The song of the Roman soldiers

(Tune: The grand old Duke of York)

Song Three: The song of the innkeepers

(Tune: Sing a song of sixpence)

Song Four: The song of the angels

(Tune: Michael row the boat ashore)

Song Five: The song of the shepherds

(Tune: Kum ba yah)

Song Six: The song of the star

(Tune: This old man)

Song Five reprise: The song of the wise men

(Tune: Kum bah yah)

APPENDIX THREE

CRAFT TEMPLATES

Lamb

Star

COMPLETING THE CRIB

Figures

Roman soldier

Angel

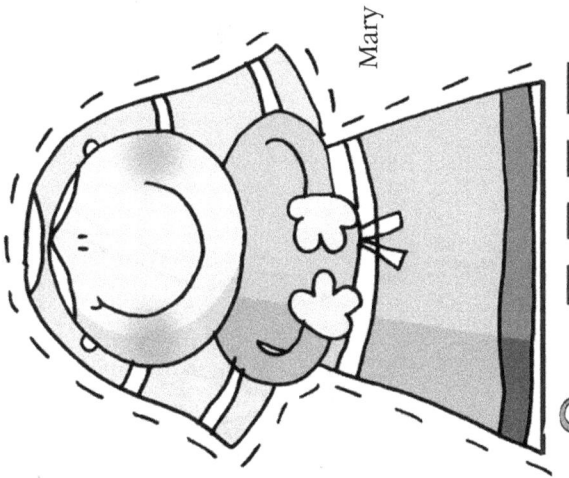

Mary

Villagers in Nazareth

Joseph

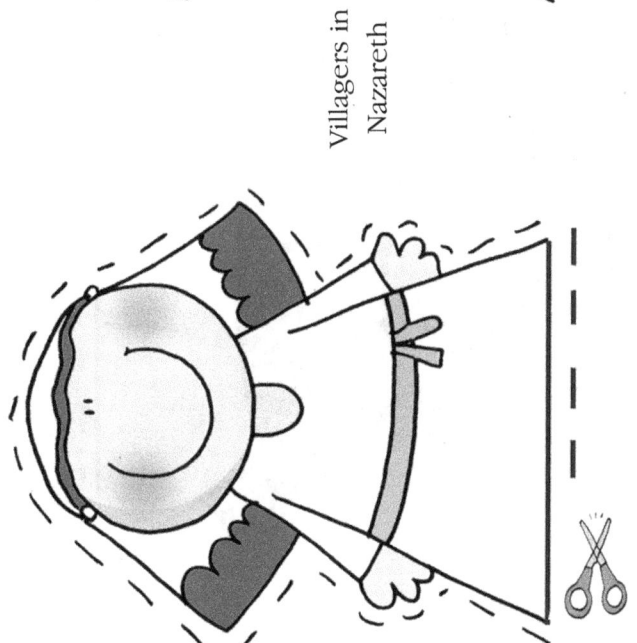

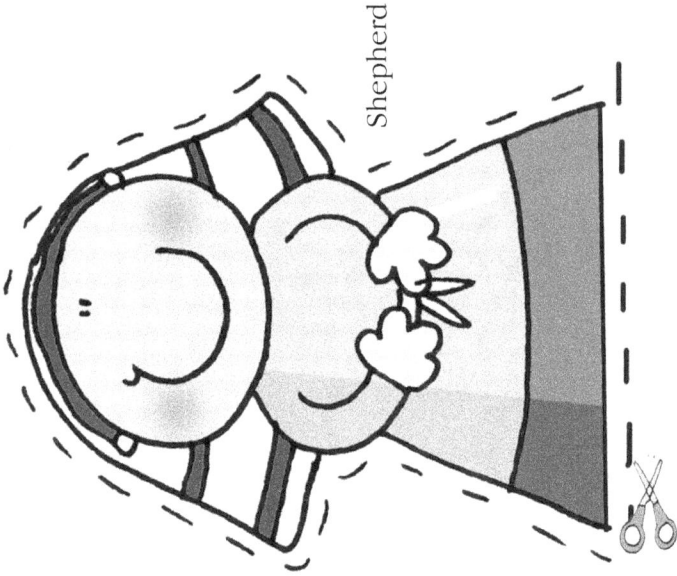

Shepherd

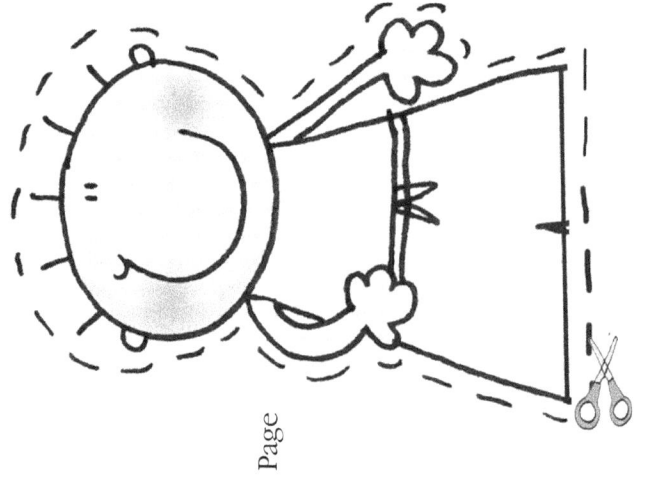

Page

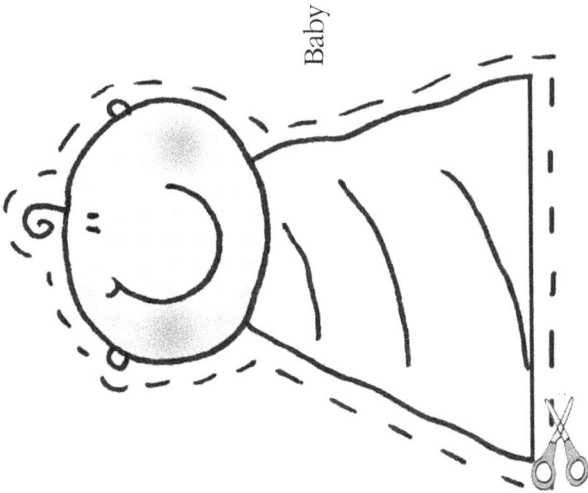

Baby

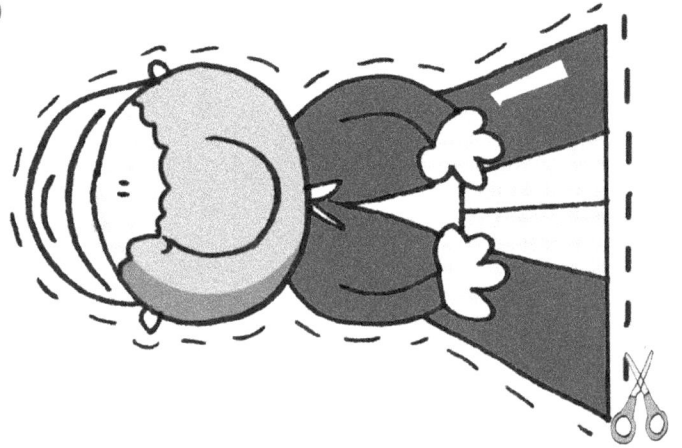

Innkeeper

Wise men

THE CHRISTMAS THREE

Dorcas

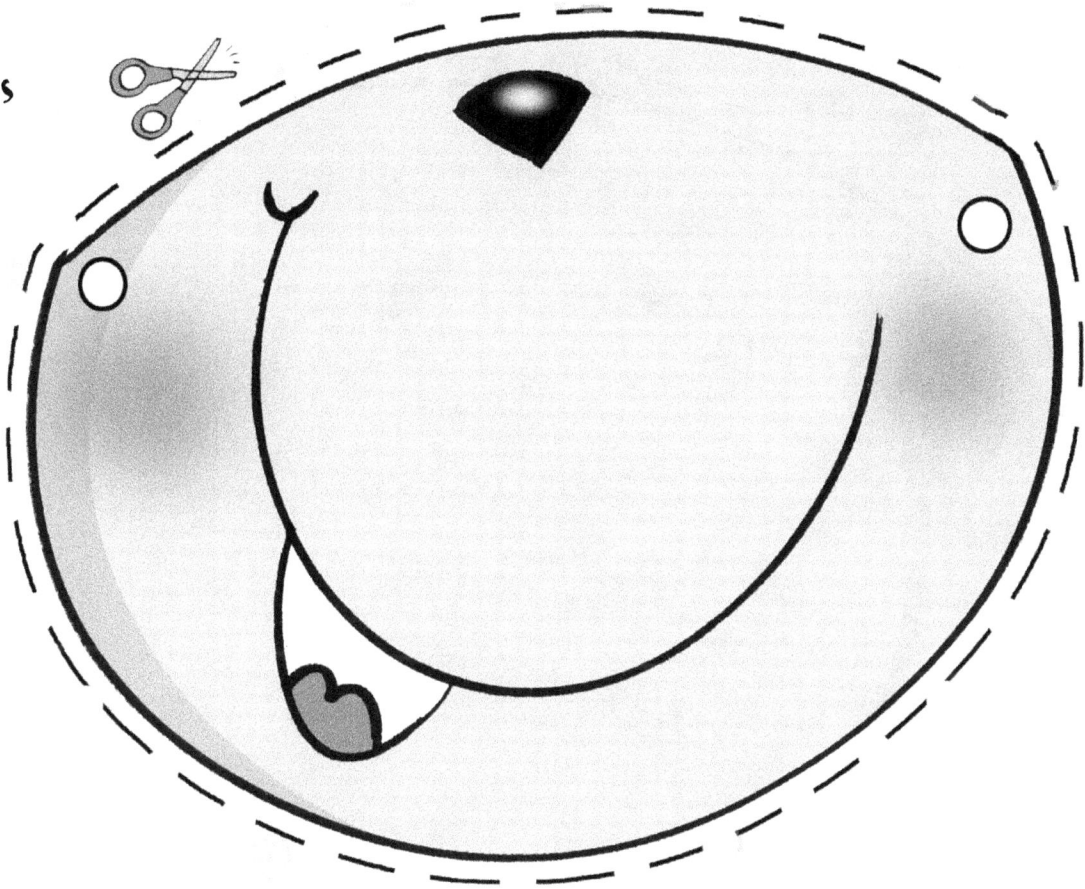

Woolly

Kasbah

Enjoyed

this book?

brf

Write a review—we'd love to hear what you think. Email: reviews@brf.org.uk

Keep up to date—receive details of our new books as they happen.
Sign up for email news and select your interest groups at:
www.brfonline.org.uk/findoutmore/

Follow us on Twitter @brfonline

By post—to receive new title information by post (UK only), complete the form below and post to: BRF Mailing Lists, 15 The Chambers, Vineyard, Abingdon, Oxfordshire, OX14 3FE

Your Details
Name _____
Address_____
_____
Town/City _____ Post Code _____
Email _____

Your Interest Groups (*Please tick as appropriate)

- ❏ Advent/Lent
- ❏ Bible Reading & Study
- ❏ Children's Books
- ❏ Discipleship
- ❏ Leadership
- ❏ Messy Church
- ❏ Pastoral
- ❏ Prayer & Spirituality
- ❏ Resources for Children's Church
- ❏ Resources for Schools

Support your local bookshop
Ask about their new title information schemes.